Russell Library
Middletown, CT 06

W9-CFV-490

SPA
J
535.6
RAN
OCT 27 2008

Children's Services
Russell Library
123 Broad Street
Middletown, CT 06457

Learn With Animals/
Aprende con los animales

Animals in Color/
Animales en color

Sebastiano Ranchetti

Reading consultant: Susan Nations, M.Ed.,
author/literacy coach/consultant
in literacy development/

Consultora de lectura: Susan Nations, M.Ed.,
autora/tutora de lectoescritura/
consultora de desarrollo de lectoescritura

WEEKLY READER®
PUBLISHING

white
polar bear

----

oso polar
blanco

3

black cat
----
gato negro

4

blue parrot

----

loro azul

6

7

serpiente roja

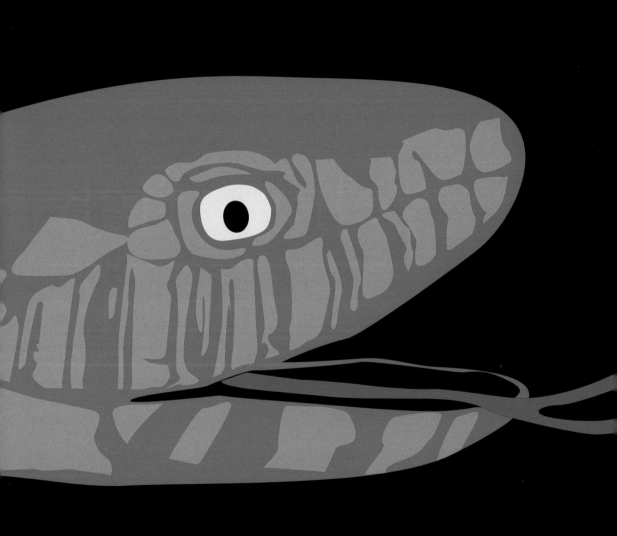

9

yellow fish
----
pez amarillo

purple
butterfly
- - - - - - - - - - -
mariposa
morada

green frog
----
rana verde

14

15

orange crab
----
cangrejo naranja

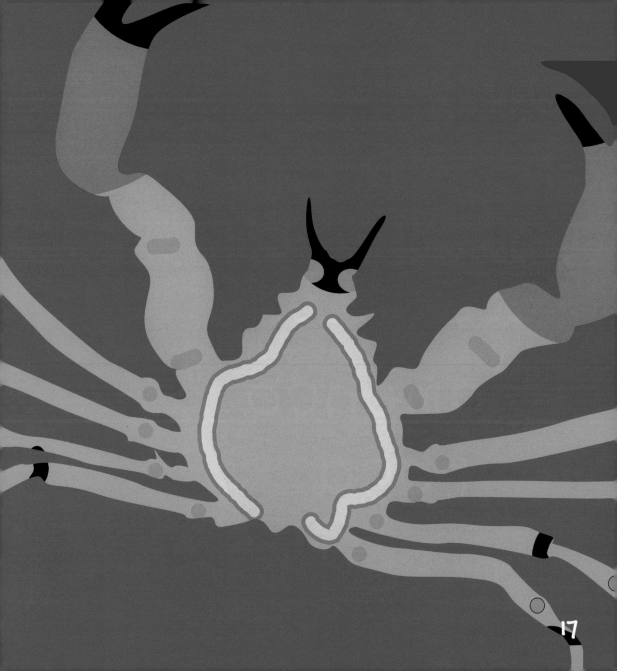

pink
flamingo
----
flamenco
rosa

19

brown
monkey

----

mono
marrón

21

white
blanco

black
negro

blue
azul

green
verde

orange
naranja

22

red
------
rojo

yellow
----
amarillo

purple
----
morado

pink
------
rosa

brown
----
marrón

23

Please visit our web site at www.garethstevens.com.
For a free color catalog describing our list of high-quality books,
call 1-800-542-2595 (USA) or 1-800-387-3178 (Canada). Our fax: 877-542-2596

Library of Congress Cataloging-in-Publication Data

Ranchetti, Sebastiano.
    [Animali a colori. Spanish & English]
    Animals in color / by Sebastiano Ranchetti = Animales en color / por
Sebastiano Ranchetti. — North American ed.
      p. cm. — (Learn with animals = Aprende con los animales)
    ISBN-10: 0-8368-9037-X   ISBN-13: 978-0-8368-9037-2 (lib. bdg.)
    ISBN-10: 0-8368-9042-6   ISBN-13: 978-0-8368-9042-6 (pbk.)
    1. Color—Juvenile literature. I. Title. II. Title: Animales en color.
  QC495.5.R3618   2008
  535.6—dc22   2007042518

This North American edition first published in 2008 by
Weekly Reader® Books
An Imprint of Gareth Stevens Publishing
1 Reader's Digest Road
Pleasantville, NY 10570-7000 USA

This U.S. edition copyright © 2008 by Gareth Stevens, Inc. International Copyright © 2006 by Editoriale Jaca Book
spa, Milano, Italy. All rights reserved. First published in 2007 as *Animali a colori* by Editoriale Jaca Book spa.

Gareth Stevens Senior Managing Editor: Lisa M. Guidone
Gareth Stevens Senior Editor: Barbara Bakowski
Gareth Stevens Creative Director: Lisa Donovan
Gareth Stevens Graphic Designer: Alexandria Davis
Spanish Translators: Tatiana Acosta and Guillermo Gutiérrez

All rights reserved. No part of this book may be reproduced, stored in a retrieval system, or transmitted
in any form or by any means, electronic, mechanical, photocopying, recording or otherwise, without the
prior written permission of the copyright holder.

Printed in the United States of America

2 3 4 5 6 7 8 9 10 09 08

About the AUTHOR and ARTIST

SEBASTIANO RANCHETTI has illustrated many books. He lives in the countryside near Florence, Italy.
His wife, three daughters, and some lively cats and dogs share his home. The ideas for his colorful
drawings come from nature and animals. He hopes his books spark your imagination!
Find out more at **www.animalsincolor.com.**

Información sobre el AUTOR/ARTISTA

SEBASTIANO RANCHETTI ha ilustrado muchos libros. Vive en el campo cerca de Florencia, Italia,
con su esposa, sus tres hijas y algunos traviesos gatos y perros. Sebastiano se inspira en
la naturaleza y los animales para sus coloridos dibujos, y espera que sus libros estimulen tu
imaginación. Para más información, visita **www.animalsincolor.com.**

A 2140 515441 6